making smart choices ™

making smart choices about
relationships

Matthew Robinson

rosen publishing's
rosen central®

New York

Published in 2008 by The Rosen Publishing Group, Inc.
29 East 21st Street, New York, NY 10010

First Edition

Library of Congress Cataloging-in-Publication Data

Robinson, Matthew, 1978–
Making smart choices about relationships / Matthew Robinson.
    p. cm.—(Making smart choices)
Includes bibliographical references.
ISBN-13: 978-1-4042-1390-6 (library binding)
1. Teenagers—Life skills guides—Juvenile literature. 2. Interpersonal relations in adolescence—Juvenile literature. 3. Choice (Psychology)—Juvenile literature. 4. Adolescent psychology—Juvenile literature. I. Title.
HQ796.R622 2008
155.5'18—dc22

                                                          2007032170

Manufactured in Malaysia

contents

introduction

Every day of your life you are faced with countless choices. In fact, nearly from the moment you open your eyes in the morning, you begin to decide what you are going to do and what you are not going to do. As you go through your day, with almost each step you take, you continue to make choices big and small. It is these choices that you make on a day-to-day basis that shape who you are as a person and who you will one day become. In many ways, the decisions you make today will play a big part in how your life will be in the future.

You could almost say that, outside of the genes passed on to you by your parents, your entire identity is based on the choices you have made and continue to make in your life. Some might be based on knowledge. For example, you choose to put an oven mitt on your hand before you pull a tray of cookies out of the oven because you have the knowledge that hot trays will burn you. Sometimes, peer pressure can play a major part in the choices you make. Maybe you take a puff off of a cigarette because everyone around you is doing it, and peer pressure has you worried they will make fun of you otherwise.

While there are many different factors that come into play when you make a choice, the bottom line is that we want the choices we make to be smart ones. By making smart choices, you can help shape yourself into the person you want to be. By making smart choices, you can help create for yourself the life you've always dreamed of.

Throughout your life, you're going to meet a lot of people. Some of them you'll meet briefly, and others will go on to become very important people in your life. The people you choose to spend time with, whether they're the ones you hang out with for just a few days or friends you keep your entire life, are people you have chosen to be in a relationship with. Some of the most important choices you will ever make will have to do with your relationships.

The people you surround yourself with can have a lot of influence over what type of experiences you have, how you behave, and even what your life will be like in the future. Just as with the other choices you make in your life, the choices you make with your relationships will be based on a variety of factors. Your choices could be based on knowledge, or they could be based on peer pressure. But just like all the choices in your life, it's important to make smart ones—especially when it comes to relationships.

This book will examine how and why you might make certain decisions regarding relationships, and it will help you learn how to make smart choices as often as possible.

Relationships come in all different shapes and sizes. Making friends and building healthy bonds can be fun, fulfilling, and exciting.

When some people think of a relationship, they think of a romantic partnership like the one that you would have with a boyfriend or a girlfriend or a spouse. In fact, the word "relationship" can be applied to lots of different partnerships in your life. You have relationships with your parents and your siblings. You have relationships with your friends. You have relationships with your teachers and your mentors. You have relationships with your boss and your coworkers. You even have relationships with your pets. (The conversations tend to be a bit one-sided, though!) As we have already said, you can also have a relationship with anyone you would consider your boyfriend, girlfriend, husband, or wife.

Anyone who plays an active or significant role in your life is someone that you have a relationship with.

Your Relationship Choices

While it is extremely important to make smart choices in your relationships, there are some relationships that you just don't have any say in. After all, you generally can't choose what parents or siblings you end up with. In regards to school, you don't have much choice as to what teacher you will get or what coach will be leading your sports team this year. If you decide to take an after-school job, outside of choosing the right job, it's not going to be up to you to pick your boss and coworkers. These are all types of relationships that, for the most part, don't fall under the category of making smart choices with relationships.

All other types of relationships—the ones you have with your friends, the ones you have with other adults (outside of family, school, and work), and your romantic relationships— are all there because you have made a choice to have those relationships in your life. This book is going to help you make smart choices both with the relationships you have now and the ones you will make in the future.

Making New Relationships

You can make a new friend almost anywhere. In fact, if you think about all the friends in your life, you will see that you have made relationships in many different ways and at many different places. Some of your relationships were made at the school where you are now. Some are from schools that you attended earlier in your life. Some relation-ships were made while participating in after-school activities. Others you made in social situations outside of school, possibly at a mall or a birthday party. You've also started relationships by making friends of your friends' friends!

You never quite know when you're going to meet someone who will play an important role in your life. It can happen almost anywhere and at any time. We're now going to break down into three different categories the many ways in which you can meet new people and form new relationships. We'll call these categories School, Organized Activities, and Social Life.

School

School is probably the best place for you to make new relationships. After all, you are there for eight hours a day with tons of kids your own age for nine or ten months out of the year. Where else does that happen? Some school relationships you make from being partnered up for class projects. Some you make by sitting together in the class-room or by eating lunch in the school cafeteria. Some relationships you make because you and your new friend share mutual interests in either an academic subject or hobby. And other relationships you make simply because you enjoy someone else's company in between classes, during recess, or at study hall.

Lots of relationships are started at school or in the classroom. Meeting someone who enjoys the same subjects as you can be a building block for a great friendship.

Organized Activities

Whether it's football or cheerleading practice after school, tae kwan do classes that your parents drive you to, summer camp, or an after-school chess or video game club that you've started with some buddies, participating in organized activities is an excellent way to form new friendships and other relationships. Some of the best buddies you'll ever have might be the ones you meet at sleepaway camp or on your school basketball team.

Social Life

Lots of relationships are developed in social situations, whether you're hanging out at the mall or at a party, or just relaxing around your parents' house with some new acquaintances. Maybe you're just hanging out at the mall with some friends and bump into a group of people from another high school and all of you start chatting. Or possibly you're walking home from school and meet another kid from your school who takes the same route home. These are just a few of the countless scenarios in which you can make new friends and start new relationships in social situations.

What to Look For

If someone comes up to you and calls you a jerk, most likely that's not going to be the start of a great relationship. Or maybe someone you're trying to start a conversation with is ignoring you or does not seem very interested. You and that person are probably not going to end up good buddies. So, what is it about your interactions with a new friend that could lead to a relationship? What exactly do you look for in a relationship? What turns someone from a stranger (or a near stranger) into a friend?

For starters, you may have a mental list of personality traits that you look for in a person. A personality trait is something about a person that separates him or her from others. For example, a sense of humor and kindness are both personality traits. A personality trait doesn't have to be positive either. Being rude or acting like a bully also can be a personality trait.

While we might not be aware of it consciously (in our minds), most likely there is a checklist of personality traits that we look for when choosing the relationships in our lives. Of course, everyone's checklist might be different. But here is an example of a list

It's important to think carefully about what type of personality traits you want or don't want in a new friend.

of personality traits that someone might look for in a new friend:

- Kindness
- Good sense of humor
- Adventurous
- Open-minded
- Positive and upbeat

On the other hand, there are personality traits that someone might want to steer clear of. Maybe these traits will be warning signs, letting you know that you don't want to have a relationship with this person:

- Overall rudeness
- Picks on others
- Intolerant of other's differences
- Bad temper
- Pressures you to do things that you don't want to do

In addition to personality traits, there are other factors involved in why you may or may not choose to have a relationship with someone. A person's hobbies, tastes, and life experiences can play a part in choosing a relationship with someone. Maybe you and your potential friend share a hobby in common, such as video games. Maybe you both like the same type of music or watch the same kind of movies. Or possibly this person has had some really interesting life experiences, such as growing up in another country, which you find very interesting, and you feel that you have a lot to learn from this new person.

Again, while everyone's checklist is different, here are a few hobbies, tastes, and life experiences that might make you consider a relationship with someone new:

- You both share a hobby that you're passionate about
- This person can teach you about things you're interested in
- This person's experiences have been different from yours, and you find that interesting

A friendship built on a common hobby, such as photography or a love of nature, can lead to countless hours of fun and learning.

- Both of you enjoy the same types of books, comic books, video games, movies, or music

On the other hand, there might be hobbies, tastes, or life experiences that you find are turnoffs when you are learning about someone new. Maybe:

- This person experiments with drugs
- This person makes fun of the hobbies you enjoy
- He or she hangs out with a dangerous group
- This person enjoys doing physically dangerous or risky activities
- You can't stand each other's tastes in books, comic books, video games, movies, or music

Putting the "Relate" in Relationship

Most of your relationships will boil down to this: you enjoy the person's company, you relate well with this person, and therefore you want to continue spending time with him or her. So, what if you enjoy someone's company, but at the same time, he or she is having a negative effect on your life? How should you feel about that? How can you tell if that is truly happening?

In the following chapters, we'll take a deeper look at relationships in terms of what you look for, how they can either be a positive or negative part of your life, and what you should do the next time you want to make a smart choice about a relationship.

chapter two

Making Smart Relationship Choices

In the previous chapter, we discussed the personality traits that someone might look for in a person when exploring a new relationship. We also discussed some of the personality traits that might make you not want to start a relationship with someone. But there's more to consider than just someone's personality when choosing to begin a relationship with him or her. Whether it's a new friend, or even a new boyfriend or girlfriend, it's important to consider all of the factors involved when making a new relationship.

In this chapter, we're going to cover different

Having fun and rocking out with your friends is important, but you've got to consider all sides when thinking about your relationships.

questions that you might find helpful to ask yourself the next time you are faced with a relationship choice. The goal of these questions is to help you consider as many factors as possible and, therefore, better your chances of making a smart choice in all of your relationships.

Making New Friends and Keeping Old Ones

Keep in mind that the questions in this chapter can be applied to both relationships that are just starting or that will start in the future, as well as relationships you already have with people. Making smart choices in your relationships isn't just about the ones you will make in the future but also about making sure the relationships you already have are right for you.

It's hard to imagine a life without your friends. They're the ones who are there for you when times are hard, and they're the ones who are with you when you're laughing and having fun. While good friends are a wonderful part of life, it is important that you decide what kind of friends that you want to have in your life. The following questions just might come in handy.

Do You Enjoy This Friend's Company?

While it may seem to be an easy question to answer at first, if you look a bit harder, you might see the question as being a bit more complicated.

Let's say that you enjoy hanging out with your friend Jane. You both laugh a lot together and like hanging out and talking with each other. But sometimes, Jane puts you down. She says things about the way you look and the way you act, and what she says makes you feel bad about yourself. Most of the time, you and Jane have a good time together, but there are times when Jane really hurts your feelings.

Or maybe you have a friend named Doug with whom you have been buddies for years. You and Doug have shared a lot of great times in the past, but lately, Doug has started to hang out with a new group of friends at school who are known to ditch classes and get into a lot of trouble. You don't want to hang out with his new friends, and Doug makes fun of you for not "being cool like these guys."

In both situations, there are things about the friend that you enjoy, but there are also things about the friend that bother you or hurt your feelings. These are important factors to take into consideration when thinking about a relationship in your life.

A Positive or Negative Influence?

A good friend can affect your life in a very positive way. He or she can fill you with self-confidence, making you feel good about yourself and helping you to achieve your goals. A good friend can help cheer you up when you're feeling down and can have fun with you when you're feeling happy. He or she wants only what is best for you. A friend like this can be a great asset to you in your life.

A friend can also affect you in a very negative way. A bad friend can wear down your self-esteem, making you feel bad about yourself and steering you away from your goals. He or she can call you names and take the wind out of your sails when you are having a good day. A bad friend is selfish. That friend only wants you to be there for him or her, and never the other way around. The friend will pressure you to do what he or she wants you to do, even if it is not the best thing for you. A friend like this can be a very negative influence in your life.

In thinking about the friends in your life, take a look at how they have influenced you. What effect have they had on your schoolwork? Have they improved or worsened your social life? How have they affected your relationship with your family? What impact did their friendship have on your goals? After you think about these questions, ask yourself, "Is this friend a positive or a negative influence in my life?"

Verbally and physically abusive relationships can have long-lasting effects on almost every aspect of your life. No one has the right to hurt you or insult you.

What Is at Stake in This Relationship?

"What is at stake in this relationship?" simply means, "What would happen in my life if this particular friend wasn't in it anymore?" Would you be happier without this friend in your life? Would you be sadder? Would you feel better about yourself without this person in your life? Would your life be worse if you didn't have this person around? These are important questions to ask yourself when you consider either making a new friend or thinking of the friends that you already have.

Romantic Relationships

A romantic relationship can be one of the most fulfilling relationships that two people can have. It can also be one of the most complicated. As you grow older, a romantic relationship can lead to wonderful things like marriage and children. Building a family with someone you love is one of the greatest paths that a relationship can take. But when you're younger and still in school, such relationships can often be confusing, stressful, or distracting.

While having a new boyfriend or girlfriend can be very exciting, it is very important that you make smart choices when it comes to your romantic relationships.

Do You Enjoy This Person's Company?

When it comes to romantic relationships, figuring out if you've made a smart choice can be unclear. Maybe you've had a crush on this person for a while, and now that he or she likes you back, you don't want anything to mess it up. But what if you find out that this person you've had a crush on is actually not as nice as you thought? Or

Having a crush on someone can be fun and exciting, as long as you don't let it distract you from the rest of your life.

what if he or she doesn't treat you the way that you want to be treated? Or, even worse, what if this person is verbally or physically abusive toward you?

In romantic relationships, you can often get "cloudy headed" when thinking about whether or not you really enjoy a person's company. After all, if you've ever had a crush on someone or felt like you were in love, then you would prefer to concentrate on the good things and not let yourself think about the bad things about that person.

While enjoying someone's company is the first building block of a romantic relationship, in order to make sure you're making smart choices, you have to ask yourself the following questions as well.

Is This Person a Positive or Negative Influence in Your Life?

Few relationships can be as distracting as romantic relationships. When you've got a new crush on someone, it can sometimes be hard to think about anything other than that crush. It can be easy to forget about important tests and homework assignments, or even after-school activities.

When you're excited about a new boyfriend or girlfriend, other relationships in your life may take a backseat. Old friends might start to wonder why you're not spending as much time with them anymore. Family members might worry that you're spending too much time with your new boyfriend or girlfriend and not enough time doing your homework or your chores.

While a romantic relationship can be fun and exciting, you have to ask yourself if it is really the right relationship for you. After all, a negative romantic relationship can affect you for the rest of your life. If you're falling behind in school or missing out on important obligations such as after-school activities or family events, then it might be time to think about the effect that your romantic relationship is having on your life as a whole.

There are also more serious types of negative influences that a romantic relationship can have on your life. Maybe your new boyfriend or girlfriend is pressuring you to try a dangerous drug or to experiment sexually. Possibly this new boyfriend or girlfriend is calling you names or making you

It's important to be open and honest with your family about your relationships. To do otherwise can lead to arguments or misunderstandings at home.

feel bad about the way you look or act. This person might be sweet to you some of the time. But if the rest of the time he or she is having a bad impact on other areas of your life, such as friends, family, and school, then you definitely should reconsider if this is the right romantic relationship for you.

What Is at Stake in This Relationship?

In order to help you make smart choices in your relationships, you must consider what things would be like with or without these people in your life. A good way to do this is to consider the pros and cons of your romantic relationship. The pros and cons will help you see both the good and the bad parts of a situation so that you can better decide if this relationship is the right one for you.

Here are some pros and cons that you might encounter in romantic relationships:

Pros:

- Your partner is nice to you.
- Your partner makes you feel good about yourself.
- You find your partner attractive.
- Your partner is supportive of other areas in your life, such as school or your hobbies.
- Your partner helps you to achieve your goals.
- Your partner is nice to your friends and family.
- Your partner respects you and your body.

Cons:

- Your partner calls you names.
- Your partner is verbally and/or physically abusive.
- Your partner hangs out with a bad crowd.
- Your partner wants you to try drugs.
- Your partner doesn't care if you fall behind in school.
- Your partner wants to keep you away from friends and family.
- Your partner tries to push you to do sexual activities.

By thinking about the pros and cons in your romantic relationships, you can come to a better understanding of what is really at stake. If the pros outweigh the cons, then this might be a good relationship for you. However, if the cons outweigh the pros, then it's time to take a serious look at your romantic relationship and how it is affecting your life.

On the Path to Making Smart Choices

Asking yourself the questions that we've covered in this chapter can put you on the right path by helping you to make smart choices in your relationships. In the following chapter, we're going to look a little farther on down that path at the possible consequences of your relationship choices.

chapter three

The Consequences of Your Choices

For every choice you make, there is a consequence. This means that for every action or decision you make, there is an end result. There are times when the consequences are good, while at other times the consequences are bad. Sometimes, they can even be a little bit of both.

The same dynamic applies to your relationship choices. For every relationship you make and every relationship you keep, you are making a choice that will have real consequences in your life. These consequences may affect your life in the present, and they may continue to affect

The people you choose to hang out with can affect your life in many ways, both positively and negatively. Choose your friends wisely.

your life far into the future. Make smart choices with your relationships as often as possible, and you will have a good chance of ending up with consequences that you will be happy with.

In this chapter, we're going to take a look at what can actually happen in your life because of your relationship choices. While we're going to look at the positive outcomes of smart relationship choices, we're also going to take a look at the more negative, scary consequences of your relationship choices.

While all would like to imagine that the friendships and romantic relationships we choose in our lives could never hurt us now or negatively affect us down the road, sadly that is not always the case. When learning to make choices in our relationships, it is really important that we take a good, long look at what can happen to us because of our choices.

Bad Friendship Choices

Not making smart relationship choices in your friendships can lead to many bad consequences. Not only can a negative friendship affect your self-esteem, your schoolwork, and your other relationships, but it can also determine your future.

The phrase "running with a bad crowd" is heard often in movies and on television. It usually means hanging out with a group of people that are into dangerous or illegal activities. You may think that you don't stand the risk of "running with a bad crowd," but what if you make a new friend who happens to spend time with people who are involved in gangs or who abuse drugs?

Sometimes when you make friends with someone, you not only enter into a relationship with that person, but you also enter into a relationship with all of his or her friends as well. Obviously, you won't know that your new friend runs with a bad crowd when you first meet him or her, but once you find out, it is your responsibility to make the right choice.

If you end up becoming friends with someone who hangs out with kids that you don't feel comfortable with, then you should let that friend know. You can say, "I like hanging out with you, but some of your other friends make me feel uncomfortable." If this person is a true friend, he or she will respect your feelings and not hold them against you.

Low Self-Esteem

Self-esteem plays a role in almost every area of your life. It's what gives you the confidence to do well in school. It's what keeps you striving for your goals. It's also what keeps you smiling and feeling good about yourself. Making the choice to have a friend in your life who makes you feel bad about yourself can have very serious and long-lasting consequences. Allowing a friend to either verbally or even physically abuse you can have a major impact on your self-esteem.

By choosing to keep such a friend, you might not try a new hobby because you're afraid of what he or she might

A real friend won't bully you, make you feel bad about yourself, call you names, or pressure you to do something you're not comfortable doing.

think or say. Your grades might even begin to slip because you start thinking that you're not smart enough to pass your tests. Even your smile seems to be missing as you walk around school all day feeling generally unhappy.

Instead of letting a friend tell you who you are, why not try telling that person that he or she needs to be supportive of you when you want to focus on your grades or try something new? Why not tell this person that if he or she were a real friend, he or she wouldn't call you names or make fun of you? A true friend will listen up and start being nicer to you.

Good Friendship Choices

A good friend will help you to become the best possible version of yourself. Your life will improve in countless ways if you make the smart choice to be friends with positive people. You will have someone to rely on in a pinch. You will have someone cheering you on from the sidelines. And, most important, you will learn how to care for someone and be there for that person when he or she needs you. Learning to be a friend for someone else can cause you to grow as a person in a number of great ways.

Real friends will be there for you when you need them, help you to feel good about yourself, and support your goals and dreams.

Bad Romantic Relationship Choices

Not making smart relationship choices can lead to disastrous results in your life. Whether you're with someone who doesn't allow you to grow as an individual, or you end up being pressured into doing something sexually that you didn't want to do, it's very important to be cautious when making choices about your romantic relationships.

Your body is yours and yours only. No matter how much you like someone, trust someone, or even love someone, no one but you has the right to make decisions about your body. If you're in a relationship with someone who is pressuring you sexually, it is important that you make it clear what your boundaries are. If someone has your best interests in mind, he or she will listen to you.

If that person doesn't listen to you, or he or she continues to pressure you into doing things with your body that you're not comfortable doing, then you need to take a close look at your romantic relationship and figure out what the smart choice is.

As a result of not making smart choices in your romantic relationships, you can end up in a situation that you never thought you'd find yourself in, like having an unwanted pregnancy or contracting a sexually transmitted disease such as AIDS.

If you don't know someone very well, then it is best to limit your interactions with that person to a public place, or around friends of yours that you know better. When you spend time alone with someone you don't know

An unplanned teen pregnancy can seriously detour all of your plans for the future. Take care of your future by being careful in your romantic relationships.

well, you open yourself up to the possibility of being raped or worse.

Someone who truly cares for you would never want to hurt you or do something to you that you're uncomfortable with. By doing your best to make smart decisions when it comes to your romantic relationships, you can help prevent negative consequences that could affect you now and in the future.

Choosing to be in a romantic relationship with someone who verbally or physically abuses you can lead to very serious consequences. Maybe the person you're with loses his or her temper one night and decides to take it out on you by either calling you names or hitting you. You choose not to do anything and instead just let it go. What happens the next time? What if you end up marrying this person and he or she unleashes anger on your future children?

It's important to know that you deserve to be in a relationship where you are never verbally or physically abused. If you are in a relationship where you fear that your partner's anger could one day spiral out of control, then you should make the choice right now to confront this person or to walk away for good.

Protect yourself and your future by making the choice to say something the first time that anything abusive happens. Don't let the consequences of someone else's anger get out of control.

A positive romantic relationship can lead to one of the most wonderful relationships that two people can experience: love, marriage, and eventually a family of your own. You'll know that you've made the smart choice in a romantic relationship when the person you're with makes you happy, respects your wishes, wants what's best for you, and supports you as you achieve your goals.

Nearly every moment in your life, you are faced with a choice: What outfit are you going to wear today? What will you eat for breakfast? Should you continue to study for the test? Who will you hang out with during lunch? Who will you take as your date to the dance on Friday night? What will you say if someone from the neighborhood asks you to join a gang? There are countless times in the day when we make choices, and each of these choices says a lot about who we are now and what we want for our futures.

Taking the time now to think long and hard about the choices you make will help you make the right choices in the future.

Each one of the instances mentioned here is a decision point. Each decision point is a moment in time when your life can go in one direction or another. Sometimes, these decision points will lead to minor changes in your life, while others will lead to major changes. Either way, every time you make a choice at a decision point, you affect your life. Therefore, every time you come to such a point, you will want to make a smart choice.

Decision Points and Relationships

Each person you meet or each relationship you keep is a decision that you make. You are always in control. It doesn't matter if the relationship is brand-new or very old. It's always up to you if you want to stay in that relationship.

If you make a new friend and he or she asks you to come to the mall and help steal some clothes, you are at a decision point in that relationship. If a very old friend of yours makes the mistake of messing around with drugs and asks you to come "get high" with him, you are at a decision point in that relationship. If you meet someone who shares your love of karate and you're wondering whether or not to invite him or her to your karate class, you are at a decision point in that relationship.

What you do at those points is up to you. As long as you keep in mind the tips and questions that we've covered in this book, you'll have a good chance of making smart choices. Remember, the smart choice is whatever choice is best for you and your future.

Learning from Your Smart Choices

Hopefully, by using the tools and ideas in this book, you will be better prepared to make smart choices when it comes to your relationships. The only way you're going to get better is by doing it.

Take a look at all of the friends in your life. Using the tools and ideas found within this book, think about these relationships and what they mean to you. Most likely, you'll find out just how many great friends you have and how much they add to your life in positive ways.

But maybe you'll find out a few things about your relationships that you want to change. Making changes in your relationships is a positive thing to do and one that can only improve your life both now and in the future.

Whether you're thinking about a friend or someone you're in a romantic relationship with, if you find things about your relationship that bother you, it's important to speak your mind. By telling the other person that there are aspects of the relationship that bother you, you give him or her the opportunity to change and to improve the relationship. If he or she doesn't listen or doesn't want to hear what you have to say, then maybe you will realize that it's a relationship that you don't need anyway.

Learning from Your Bad Choices

While it's important to make smart decisions as often as possible, no one is perfect. Everyone makes relationship mistakes sometimes. After all, having trust in people is a

Knowing you've made the right choices in your friendships is priceless. Almost as priceless as having a lifelong friend you know you can count on.

positive personality trait. Some people are going to hurt you or disappoint you, and there will have been no way for you to see it coming. That's life.

The only way to learn is to make mistakes. The more you learn about what you enjoy or don't enjoy in a relationship, the better equipped you will be for the next relationship you have. Relationships are great for learning about other people, but they are just as good for learning about yourself.

Learning about yourself and others is a big part of a healthy relationship. Now get out there and have fun with the people you love and who love you.

Enjoy Your Relationships

There are few things as great on this planet as a good relationship. Whether it's a relationship with a family member, a friend, a mentor, your boyfriend or girlfriend, or your husband or wife, a good relationship is priceless.

So, get out there, make smart choices in your relationships, and don't forget to let those with whom you have good relationships know just how much they mean to you.

glossary

acquaintance Someone you know but whom you are not close with.

boundaries Rules you have set for yourself that you don't want others to break, like rules about your body.

consciously Being aware of; doing something on purpose.

consequence The result of an action or inaction.

genes The building blocks of our DNA, which decide everything from eye color to height.

identity Everything about you, including your name, your appearance, and your personality.

influence Something or someone that affects you in some way; to have an effect on.

interaction An instance of communicating with someone, whether verbally or nonverbally.

obligation Something that you must do, such as completing a homework assignment or showing up for an after-school activity.

peer pressure When peers (people who are your age or in your social group) try to convince you to do things that you are uncomfortable with.

personality traits Descriptions of a person's moods or behaviors, like funny or serious.

relationship A bond between people.

scenarios Situations in which an event unfolds.

sibling A brother or sister.

spouse A husband or wife.

for more
information

CORA (Community Overcoming Relationship Abuse)
P.O. Box 5090
San Mateo, CA 94402
(650) 652-0800
Web site: http://www.corasupport.org
CORA is a resource for people who are suffering from or
  looking for information about relationship abuse.

Leave Out Violence (LOVE)
1015 Atwater Avenue
Montreal, QC H3H 1X4
Canada
(514) 938-0006
Web site: http://www.leaveoutviolence.com
LOVE is a Canadian organization dedicated to preventing
  domestic abuse, including relationship violence and
  teen violence.

National Youth Violence Prevention
P.O. Box 10809
Rockville, MD 20849-0809
(866) 723-3968

Web site: http://www.safeyouth.org

National Youth Violence Prevention is an organization
    aimed at stopping teen violence of all kinds, including
    gang violence.

Planned Parenthood Federation of America
434 West 33rd Street
New York, NY 10001
(212) 541-7800
Web site: http://www.plannedparenthood.org
Planned Parenthood offers information about birth control
and preventing sexually transmitted diseases.

Public Health Agency of Canada
130 Colonnade Road, A.L. 6501H
Ottawa, ON K1A 0K9
Canada
(613) 946-0879
Web site: http://www.phac-aspc.gc.ca
The Public Health Agency of Canada is a government
    resource that provides information on teen relationships
    and teen health.

Substance Abuse and Mental Health Services
    Administration (SAMHSA)
1 Choke Cherry Road
Rockville, MD 20857
(240) 276-2000

Web site: http://www.samhsa.gov
SAMHSA is a great place to get tons of information about
    maintaining healthy relationships when substance
    abuse or mental health issues are involved.

Web Sites

Due to the changing nature of Internet links, Rosen
Publishing has developed an online list of Web sites
related to the subject of this book. This site is updated
regularly. Please use this link to access the list:

http://www.rosenlinks.com/msc/rela

for further reading

Bell, Ruth. *Changing Bodies, Changing Lives: A Book for Teens on Sex and Relationships.* New York, NY: Times Books, 1998.

Canfield, Jack. *Chicken Soup for the Teenage Soul on Love & Friendship.* Deerfield Beach, FL: Health Communications, 2002.

Kirberger, Kimberly. *On Relationships: A Book for Teenagers.* Deerfield Beach, FL: Health Communications, 1999.

Macavinta, Courtney. *Respect: A Girl's Guide to Getting Respect and Dealing When Your Line Is Crossed.* Minneapolis, MN: Free Spirit Publishing, 2005.

Mayall, Beth. *Get Over It! How to Survive Breakups, Back-Stabbing Friends, and Bad Haircuts.* New York, NY: Scholastic, 2000.

Middleman, Amy B., and Kate Gruenwald Pfeifer. *American Medical Association Boy's Guide to Becoming a Teen.* San Francisco, CA: Jossey-Bass, 2006.

Price, Elizabeth. *Divorce and Teens: When a Family Splits Apart.* Berkeley Heights, NJ: Enslow Publishing, 2004.

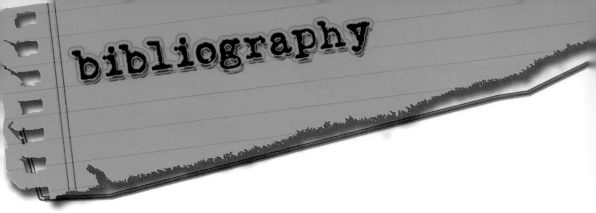

bibliography

Basso, Michael J. *The Underground Guide to Teenage Sexuality: The Essential Handbook for Today's Teens and Parents.* Minneapolis, MN: Fairview Press, 2003.

Grevious, Saundrah Clark. *Teen Smart! Ready-to-Use Activities to Help Teens Build Positive Relationships with Peers and Adults.* San Francisco, CA: Jossey-Bass, 1999.

Kelsey, Candice M. *Generation MySpace: Helping Your Teen Survive Online Adolescence.* New York, NY: Marlowe & Co., 2007.

Miron, Amy G. *How to Talk with Teens About Love, Relationships & S-E-X: A Guide for Parents.* Minneapolis, MN: Free Spirit Publishing, 2002.

Murray, Jill. *But I Love Him: Protecting Your Teen Daughter from Controlling, Abusive Dating Relationships.* New York, NY: ReganBooks, 2000.

Weill, Sabrina Solin. *The Real Truth About Teens & Sex: From Hooking Up to Friends with Benefits: What Teens Are Thinking, Doing, and Talking About and How to Help Them Make Smart Choices.* New York, NY: Perigee, 2005.

index

About the Author

Matthew Robinson has mentored and tutored kids and teens all across the country. Married since November 2007 to a woman he loves very much, Robinson understands the importance of healthy, strong relationships.

Photo Credits

Cover, p. 18 © www.istockphoto.com; pp. 6, 9 © www.istockphoto.com/Chris Schmidt; p. 11 © www.istockphoto.com/Rosemarie Gearhart; p. 13 © Myleen Ferguson Cate/Photo Edit; p. 15 © www.istockphoto.com/Li Kim Goh; p. 20 © www.istockphoto.com/Jacob Wackerhusen; p. 22 © Michael Newman/Photo Edit; p. 25 © Will Hart/Photo Edit; p. 28 © Kayte M. Deioma/Photo Edit; p. 29 © www.istockphoto.com/Sean Locke; p. 31 © Robert Brenner/Photo Edit; p. 34 © David Young-Wolff/Photo Edit; p. 37 © www.istockphoto..com/Maartje van Caspel; p. 38 © www.istockphoto.com/Justin Harrocks.

Designer: Tahara Anderson; **Editor:** Nicholas Croce
Photo Researcher: Marty Levick

DATE DUE